Single Minded

~≈~

Bishop Kenneth W. Paramore, DMin

Copyright © 2018
by Bishop Kenneth W. Paramore, DMin

Single Minded
by Bishop Kenneth W. Paramore, DMin

Printed in the United States of America

ISBN: 978-0-692-12312-6

All rights reserved. No part of this document may be reproduced or transmitted in any form, by any means (electronic, photocopying, recording, or otherwise) without the written permission of the author.

Unless otherwise indicated, Bible quotations are taken from the King James Version of the Bible.

Published by:
Highly Recommended Int'l, Gail Dudley
1491 Polaris Parkway, #81
Columbus, Ohio 43240 USA
www.GailDudley.com
www.ReadyPublication.com

Cover Art:
Walthall Wood Jr
BOMBSHELL WORLDWIDE

Dedication

To the Body

There are too many names to list individually.
To Christ Centered Church East and
Christ Centered Church West, thank you
for supporting me through this work.
To all of my friends, brothers, mentors, sons,
daughters, mothers, fathers, and family,
thank you for praying me through.

To Ma and Dad
James E. and Betty J. Paramore
We're writing books now…

This work is dedicated to you.

Table of Contents

Introduction		vii
Chapter 1	Knowing Yourself	11
Chapter 2	You're Saved	17
Chapter 3	You're Sanctified	27
Chapter 4	You're Satisfied	35
Chapter 5	Sexuality…Sinful or Sacred?	41
Chapter 6	What Turns Me On	49
Chapter 7	If Walls Could Talk!	59
Chapter 8	Saving All My Love	65
Chapter 9	Has Anybody Seen "Do Right"?	71
Chapter 10	Decision Time	77
About the Author		85

Introduction

I have been preaching for thirty years and I have been a senior pastor for twenty-six years. The one thing I have found constant in pastoral ministry is that overall we as Christians have no idea how to establish, develop, and sustain a romantic relationship.

The age does not matter; neither does gender. We typically do not understand the dynamic of romantic relationship. What most do in the best effort is just agree to live unfulfilled in their relationships or terminate a relationship that could very well be a gift from God.

It is my personal belief that we need more Bible-based, honest, and real material to help people not merely stay married, but also how to establish, develop, and sustain romantic covenant relationships that are both fulfilling and that give God the glory in their existence.

I should mention now that I have been with the same woman for over thirty-two years, but we have not been happily married for the whole while. It took some years for us to get there. The reason for this is because our relationship was birthed at a time in the church and ministry where the words, "It is better to marry than to burn" were taken maniacally out of context. Many in my generation believed that to honor God and be in ministry we needed to be married. The problem with this is that there was really no mentoring or counseling going on to teach what marriage would ultimately be like.

We got married with Holy Ghost blinders on, believing that somewhere between Bible study, Sunday school, worship services, revivals, tithing, fasting, and praying, somehow the relationship would work. We believed this only to find out that we had been sold a bill of goods. We found out that loving God and even loving another human being does not necessarily mean that you will have a mutually fulfilling and productive relationship.

Many of us who were married at that time struggled and got divorced and remarried and divorced again because we still could not figure out the relationship dynamic. Flash forward thirty years to this

Introduction

present age of relationship and establishing, developing, and sustaining a romantic relationship is even more difficult than it was three decades ago.

There are so many distractions. There are so many options. There are so many versions of Christian love and romance being promoted and experienced that it is now very difficult to tell what way is the right way. It seems that now we simply make up the relationship rules as we go.

This work is being done to help those who still desire a biblical and yet fulfilling and exciting romantic relationship with the man or woman of their dreams. These types of relationships are not hit or miss. These types of relationships are not mythical and premised in fantasy. These relationships can be achieved if in fact we are willing to put the time into both understanding them and ultimately establishing, developing, and sustaining one.

I am reaching out for those who desire this because no one was there for us when we got started with any information that could really help us. Therefore, over the next few pages I will share with you what God has given me, what I have learned, and what I have stumbled upon in hopes that you will avoid the trouble that we have survived trying to get to this place in our life and our marriage.

This information should not be given after the fact of marriage, but this information should be given while the parties are yet single. So, here we go....

First things first.... How do you feel about you?

Chapter 1

Knowing Yourself

Love is perhaps the most complicated thing a person will encounter in a lifetime. I say this because while it is one thing, it is also a plethora of things. Love is an emotion in that one can feel loved, yet it is a state of mind. Love is a fantasy, yet it is a reality. Love is giving, yet it is also receiving. We could go on and on like this concerning what love is without ending. However, there is one thing that cannot be argued or debated and that is love is knowledge.

We can only truly love that which we experience or know. True love requires acquaintance. Love requires us to become acquainted and familiar with the object of our affection. Knowledge is key because true love is unselfish and undying. It is only through the knowledge of the one who is the object of our affection that we can offer them what it is they need. Many are confused on the issue, but love for an individual can only really be shown through how much we are willing to meet their needs. What we are willing to do for them to make their lives better becomes the litmus test for love. Then and only then can we move to any action that can be mutually meaningful for both parties.

> *John 3:16*
> *For God so loved the world, that he gave his only begotten Son, that whosoever believeth in him should not perish, but have everlasting life.*

It is important for us to understand in the quest for love what love is supposed to do. Nothing makes that clearer for a believer than John 3:16. The verse is very exact in what it is that love does.

1. Love is overwhelming. (God so loved)
2. Love chooses where it goes. (The world)
3. Love is about the other person. (He gave)
4. Love makes the recipient better. (They don't perish)
5. Love is forever…if it's real. (Everlasting)

However, this whole procedure becomes impossible if a person has not learned to love him/herself first.

If a person does not love themselves, they usually enter a relationship looking for someone to validate them. They are looking for the other person to be responsible for making them feel happy or whole. Immediately when this happens the priority of love, which is service, is placed on the back burners for that person to fulfill their own deficits. When a person has not learned to love self, when they enter into a relationship they can only be selfish. Instead of showing love their focus is on being shown love. We must love ourselves before entering any human relationship. If we don't, we will merely pimp that person for our own emotional gain.

Now that we have already mentioned to you that love comes from knowledge, in the next section I would like to introduce you to you. Once a person can love themselves they become much more attractive, confident, and able to love someone other than themselves. More importantly, there is less chance of them lowering their standards, compromising, accepting abuse, and depending on the other person, for giving and sustaining significance.

Things You Should Know About You

You're Special!

It is imperative to know as an individual that you are special. To say that one is special is to say that they are unique, different, and important. YOU'RE SPECIAL!

Psalm 139:14
I will praise thee; for I am fearfully and wonderfully made: marvelous are thy works; and that my soul knoweth right well.

Facts About You

- God created you the best. (You are perfectly you.)
- There's no one else like you in the whole world. (DNA)
- There's a divine purpose that only you can fulfill. (God has a purpose for you.)
- Though you are not faultless, you are flawless. (Your faults are how God gets His glory out of you. They are not flaws...they are perfectly placed imperfections [2 Corinthians 4:7].)

Once we realize that God has made us special we become special to ourselves. When we view ourselves as special we will demand a certain level of special treatment. We will also realize that it does not take a man or woman outside of ourselves to give us our significance. We realize that our significance comes from God.

Chapter 1 Quiz

1. How can I know I truly love someone?

   _____
   _____
   _____
   _____
   _____
   _____

2. Why am I special?

   _____
   _____
   _____
   _____
   _____

3. Why should I not allow myself to be mistreated?

   _____
   _____
   _____
   _____
   _____

Chapter 2

You're Saved

We were special long before we were saved. God made us special for HIM. God has arranged salvation for us.

I believe one of the greatest faults of the church is that we have allowed people to come into this faith without actually knowing what salvation is. We have focused on filling the pews rather than filling hearts with the Good News of the Gospel of Jesus Christ. Most pastors are very big on membership, but not discipleship.

Being a member of the church has never made anyone a better person. That can only happen if we allow ourselves to be disciplined in the things of Christ Jesus. It is at that point we become a disciple. Quite frankly, disciples think far more differently than members.

When we are not discipled, we become guilty of professing Christianity, but living in carnality. Because we live in carnality we constantly live beneath the place in life that God has for us. Many of us lose the joy of our salvation through compromising, lowering standards, not having expectations, and suffering moral and spiritual defeat. For a single person there is nothing more important than the joy of your salvation.

As singles, there are times when you will go through some very trying ordeals. You can go through ordeals that are specific to being a single person and they can be devastating if you don't understand your salvation. The inverse of this is true as well. Because you do understand your salvation, there will be some ordeals that you will never experience.

Salvation keeps us when we cannot keep ourselves. Because we are humans there are some things that we crave. The things that we crave are not bad; however, to pursue them as a single person can place us in a bad spiritual predicament. These cravings can easily pull us out of the will of God, therefore making it difficult for God to bless us the way He desires to. For this cause your salvation works to guide you, to protect you, and to restore you.

Salvation is there to guide us down the right paths in life. Once we find the path, salvation is there to protect us while we are on the path. Salvation is also there to restore us when we fall. There is no way you will live the single experience and never fall down. But there is also no way when you fall you should stay down as a child of God.

I want to apologize for the church of the previous generation, of which I am a product. We promoted a lot of things that have crippled the church as it relates to relationships, family, marriage, and dating.

We perpetuated that Jesus was enough! While Jesus is enough to save you, you will need more than just being saved to navigate through the murky waters of singlehood. My generation just lived two lives. We acted holy in front of those we did not want to disappoint or those who could execute punishment, but we lived another way with our peers. All this did was make us severely hypocritical in our witness for the Lord.

I am fifty years old. Many people who are my age and older that got saved at a young age have suffered from severe marital problems, if not being divorced several times all together. They gave us church rhetoric instead of mentoring and truth. We were extremely dysfunctional in our relationships because they were premised in pretention. We simply pretended that we were not hot and bothered. We pretended that we were not sexually active. We pretended that we were not going out and experiencing all manner of lifestyles. We pretended because no one prepared us how to live through it and confront it successfully.

No one taught us how to deal with what we were craving. Times have changed, but basic human craving has not. You all are still craving what we craved.

Seven Cravings of a Single Saint

1. Companionship
2. Social Life
3. Sex
4. Stability
5. Confidante
6. Understanding
7. Conversation/Meaningful Dialogue

Companionship

No one really wants to spend their life alone. Everyone craves that special someone to be with in a mutually exclusive relationship that is both fulfilling and productive. While there are exceptions to this rule, meaning there are some people who just prefer to be single, the majority of people who say they choose to be single are only doing so because they have been perpetually unsuccessful at relationships and love.

Social Life

Social life is a big deal for a young adult and in many cases mature adults who find themselves "single again." The church has been very deficient in providing opportunities for socializing among the single population. It is not my suggestion that all social events have to be about getting people "booed up," but we should take on the responsibility of at least providing regular opportunities for social interaction. Sitting at home can be very depressing. It often pushes the single saint to go into the world for entertainment and socialization because the church will not provide anything.

Sex

We can play if we want to, but sex is not of the devil—sex is of God. It is His gift to us. It is a beautiful thing to feel intimate attraction towards another human being. However, we cannot punish this and penalize this. We must learn how to prepare our singles and our young people to deal with this. God's Word will always be true, but we still need dialogue, help, mentoring, and transparency to successfully equip our singles to manage this craving. It is my belief that as early as middle school the church should engage in this dialogue because they are already having it in school.

Stability

Singles get to a certain place where they want to settle down. They want to have a permanent address. They want to have a career. That want to have all things that substantiate them as an adult. The key is they also need to know what type of people can help them achieve this and what kind of people will hinder achieving the stability they desire. Them being attractive does not make them an asset in your life.

Confidante

Everyone needs someone to talk to. Someone they can tell everything and know they will be neither judged nor abandoned. Many will develop this relationship with someone other than their romantic interest. However, a true soul mate should be one you can bare your soul to and not have to worry about repercussion or judgment. Hard to find…hard to find.

Understanding

We crave someone that gets us. You need someone that understands who you are as a person and they are all right with who you are as a person. You do not need anyone to change you. You need someone who will assist you in your development as you assist them in theirs. This can only come through understanding.

Conversation/Meaningful Dialogue

We crave someone who loves to hear our voice. You need to be in a relationship with someone who loves to hear you. Not just the timber and tonality of your voice, but they love to hear *you*. They love to hear your thoughts, opinions, ideas, and disagreements because they value your person, your intellect, and emotion as the greatest part of your person. You should not have to hide these to get along.

If any of these cravings are unmet in a relationship, that relationship has great potential to become unbalanced and ultimately dysfunctional. These cravings are essential to every human being. What is important is that we don't drop our standards to have a craving temporarily fulfilled. We have to be developed to understand it is possible to meet "a person" who can satisfy all of these cravings, but we have to be willing to do the same thing for the person who does it for us.

This is something that cannot be rushed. We have to take our time and allow it to develop. This is necessary because we want to be able to keep what is developed and not have to throw it out or put it back because it will not suffice in fulfilling our need. In the meantime, here are some Scriptures to build you up while you are preparing for your relationship.

Scriptures That Bring Life

When you need encouragement… Isaiah 43:1-4
When you need reassuring… Psalm 23
When you need to know you're provided for…Matthew 6:33
When you need peace…John 16:33
When you need to be humbled…Romans 3:23
When you need to shout…Romans 6:23
When you need to recover…Romans 7:21-25
When you need validation…Romans 8 (all of it!)
When you need to check yourself…
1 Corinthians 6:19
When you need to extinguish a fire…
1 Corinthians 7:9

When you need to make a comeback...
1 Corinthians 6:14
When you need the truth...2 Corinthians 6:14
When you need to be pushed...Philippians 4:13
When you need to be reminded...
Philippians 4:19

Amen.

Chapter 2 Quiz

1. What is Salvation?

2. What is Discipleship?

3. What do you crave most in relationships?

Chapter 3

You're Sanctified

Sanctification is the setting apart of a people for holy and specific purposes. I sincerely believe that there is both a holy and a specific purpose for the circumstance that is known as singlehood.

I understood sanctification in theory as a pastor and a doctor of the church, but the best illustrational definition I have ever received for sanctification came from the wisdom of my deacon's ministry chairman, who had never spent a day in a seminary. He described sanctification by sharing with us the process they would use in his hometown in Mississippi to prepare a hog for slaughter.

He said they would single out the animal they wanted for an event, maybe a holiday, and then they would separate it from the rest of the pigs. They would not set it in the mud with the rest of the pigs but had an elevated stand it would stay on. It would not eat the regular slop that was fed the regular pig because it was on a special diet because it had been chosen for a purpose. Finally, when the pig was fat enough they would then take it out and slaughter it for the benefit of the family.

That's the same way that God sanctifies us. Once we become His, He identifies us and sets us apart from everyone else. We are no longer allowed to wallow in the places we used to wallow in because we now have purpose. He elevates us and He makes sure that all of our needs are met. He is not doing this for us because He wants us to appear to be better than all the rest. He is doing this because ultimately, He wants to use us. He wants us to sacrifice ourselves for His service. He wants us to give ourselves for the good of the rest of the Body of Christ. Ladies and gentlemen, this is sanctification.

So many times people who are single view it as a curse. To the contrary, it is actually a blessing. On at least two occasions the apostle Paul stated how marriage can hinder a Christian's work in the ministry for the Lord (1 Corinthians 7). From this we see that being single is a type of sanctification for the glory of God. Therefore, while I am single I am not on a perpetual quest to end my singlehood, but I am more so on a quest to fulfill my capacity to serve God in this season of my life.

What we are not teaching the single population in the Body of Christ is that singlehood is in and of itself an assignment. It is an assignment that when completed will bring promotion.

It is my sincere belief that if a man or a woman desires a husband or a wife and prepares themselves to be the spouse of the one they desire, God will grant them the desire of their heart. However, that person must complete their assignment in their season of singlehood in order to get that promotion.

To illustrate this let's look at Adam in the garden of Eden. We have repeatedly taught that God gave Adam a wife because when Adam saw all the other animals coupled up it made him feel some type of way and God didn't want that, so He blessed Adam with a mate of his own. This is perhaps one of the worst theological explanations we have ever given on anything coming out of the Bible.

The truth of the matter is, Adam did not look at animals and think of love. Number one, that would be bestiality; and number two, he had no idea that he was built for someone because everything Adam needed to survive in the garden he already was. In fact, so perfect was Adam in his singlehood that God didn't say that he was just good, but He said

Adam was very good. He then gave Adam assignments that he had to fulfill. Adam had to establish order in his garden before anything else could go further.

We have to stop wanting and asking God to send people into our chaos before we have brought order into our garden. Exes, babies' moms and babies' dads, poverty, unemployment, and lack of planning are things that do not reflect the goodness of God in one's life. If these things plague your life, why would God send anyone who has prayed for someone into it?

Adam completed his assignment as a single man and then God said it was not good for him to be alone. God self-declared that it was time for Adam to have someone. It was not because Adam was lonely, but it was because God said, "Let Me take you to the next phase of your existence. I have another assignment for you because you have completed the first with flying colors. The next part, however, will call for you to have a partner. You will not be able to do the next part on your own. I will give you help."

As a single person, embrace your singlehood and complete every assignment with excellence while you are single. God desires to bring someone into excellence, not chaos. When they come in it should be clear what the next part of your life together will be about. God does not put people together for the purpose of sex, home ownership, children, and traveling. God puts people together so that He can be glorified by their union.

To this end, you are not looking for someone to have a good time with, but you are looking for someone to have dominion with so you can subdue your surroundings and give God the glory out of your union. To produce this God has to sanctify you or set you apart first in preparation for you sacrificing your singlehood for marriage.

Please, as a single person, do not neglect to see that you are in a very special time and place in your life. Do not despise yourself in this season, but embrace yourself and get to know yourself. The only reason that God has sanctified you from a relationship is to ultimately prepare you for a relationship. Live in excellence and allow your excellence to draw your help to you.

Questions to Ask Yourself While You Are Set Apart

1. Have I made Christ the center of my life?
2. Am I ready to sacrifice myself to and for a relationship?

3. What do I have to bring into a relationship that is beneficial to the other person?
4. Am I capable of putting someone before myself?
5. Can I meet the relationship needs of a person emotionally, physically, and most all spiritually?

Chapter 3 Quiz

1. What does it mean to be Sanctified?

2. What am I set apart for?

3. What should I be looking for in a mate/companion?

Chapter 4

You're Satisfied

Philippians 4:11
Not that I speak in respect of want: for I have learned, in whatsoever state I am, therewith to be content.

It is of the utmost importance for us to understand that this season of singlehood will be our season until God decides to change it. As believers we have to understand that things happen to us for two reasons: they either happen by consequence, or they happen by design.

As a believer it is important to remember that the steps of a good man or woman are ordered by the Lord (Psalm 37:23). This means that as a believer I don't show up anywhere on my journey by happenstance or accident. God is always ordering my steps.

There are times when my steps are ordered because of consequences. In other words, I have lived my life in such a way where the actions that I have taken in my life have now caused a very specific reaction that I am going to have to deal with. It is the Law of Reciprocity: I have sown this, so I must reap this harvest. Consequences can have us in places that we would rather not be in. However, if this is your reality, you have to know and believe that if you change your sowing habits, you will also change your harvesting. You do not have to stay in any situation that you are in; you can always decide to sow your way out.

To do this it requires a person to begin to do things God's way instead of your way. As you are sowing, remember, it took you a while to get the consequences you are dealing with; it could take a little while to sow your way out. Just remember that God is indeed faithful and His Word does not lie. Start sowing your way into better company, better relationships, and better habits and watch how much different your harvest will become.

The other way we end up in places is by design. This means that we have been in the will of God and because of that we are in the place that He literally has designed for us to be in. We have walked in His Word and will to the best of our ability, and favor has gotten us in the place that we are now occupying.

Sometimes when we see people getting married and we never even saw them dating or with anyone of the opposite sex, we scratch our heads in disbelief and wonder, *How did that happen?* They're not really the cutest. They're not really the most fashionable. They're not really even the best built. So then how did they land such an awesome soul mate? There is only one reason. It has been done by design. God's favor is given to anyone who purposes in their heart to do it God's way.

This is not a matter of perfection. This is a matter of persistence. I continued to try my level best to do it God's way and because of that He has had favor upon me.

Now, if you are in consequence, please do not worry about it. Remember, just change your sowing habits and your harvest will change as well. Also, remember that no matter where you are or what's going on, God's Word is true:

Romans 8:28
And we know that all things work together for good to them that love God, to them who are the called according to his purpose.

Finally, we must realize that being satisfied does not mean that we are complacent. It does not mean that we lack aspiration or desire. To be satisfied means that I am okay where I am even if I truly prefer to be somewhere else. I will not allow my desire to be in another place make me hate the place that God has blessed me in or is keeping me in right now. In fact, to show God that I appreciate Him, I will thank Him every day for where I am even as I plan to leave this place for where I desire to be.

To this end, it creates a strategy for me to live by even in my singlehood. I am praising Him like I made it, but I'm planning and working like it's on the way. I find my comfort both in the praise and in the work.

While I am working, I am also waiting because I do not want another counterfeit blessing. I need my next relationship to be fashioned in heaven and forged in favor. I need to be sweetly sure that God has done it for me because I have no desires to do it again. Therefore, I'll wait.

Isaiah 40:31

But they that wait upon the L*ord* *shall renew their strength; they shall mount up with wings as eagles; they shall run, and not be weary; and they shall walk, and not faint.*

Chapter 4 Quiz

1. How did you get to this place in your life?

   _____
   _____
   _____
   _____

2. What does being Satisfied mean?

   _____
   _____
   _____

3. Why should I learn to wait?

   _____
   _____
   _____

4. What is the importance of Sowing?

   _____
   _____
   _____
   _____

Chapter 5

Sexuality...Sinful or Sacred?

There are certain things that are taboo in terms of discussion among Christians. There are things we don't like to talk about, and if we do talk about them, we don't do it with any level of true transparency. Perhaps the most monumental of all of these issues is that of sexuality.

Sexuality is not to be confused with sex. There is a distinct difference between the two. Most of us are fully knowledgeable of the sex act itself (intercourse). However, we have not really grasped an understanding of our sexuality.

Am I homosexual, heterosexual, or asexual? Am I reserved or am I outgoing? Am I private or am I voyeuristic? These are just a few of the questions that every believer needs to ask and answer concerning themselves before we would get involved in any committed and/or romantic experience that involves the feelings, hopes, and well-being of another person.

In this chapter, sexuality will be defined as:

One's character, disposition, and attitude as it relates to sex. A comprehensive knowledge of one's sexual preference, practices, and pleasures. A total understanding of one's self sexually.

To live victorious as a saved, single individual it is imperative that every believer knows, recognizes, identifies, and admits their sexuality. It is only by doing these things that we prevent getting ourselves into sinful, compromising, and embarrassing situations.

So, let us begin the discussion by saying that sexuality is not a "bad thing." In fact, it is a gift from God. Scripture is very clear in the book of James that every good and every perfect gift comes from God. The problem that we so often have is that perfect gifts should never be placed in unprepared hands.

We are notorious for becoming sexual before we understand our sexuality. When this happens, every person we encounter becomes a type of on-the-job training for us. We are oftentimes reckless and inconsiderate as we leave a trail of unsuspecting, wounded people in our aftermath of sexual awakening.

Please be fully aware that God wants us to both experience and enjoy sex. However, He wants us to do this in the parameters of holiness that He has set for us. He does not want us to rewrite Scripture. He does not want us to do away with theology simply because it is more difficult to execute in this present age. He desires for us to enjoy it, but to do it His way. This has been His will from the beginning.

In the book of Genesis, chapter 2, Adam's statement concerning Eve is one of pleasure and genuine excitement. He does not view Eve and say, "Hey." No, when Adam sees his mate for the first time he says, "This is bone of my bone and flesh of my flesh." He recognizes her as being made just for him.

The theology in this is profound. Adam is aware that everything he has had dominion over and given names to had come in pairs. He has noticed that nothing in Eden looked like him. Therefore, when God gave him something that was just for him, it created an excitement and demanded an acknowledgement. To this end, when we meet someone, it should not be someone that we are simply sampling, but we should wait for the testimony of our total man that says, "This person has been both fashioned and forwarded to me by both the hand and will of God."

If we don't wait for this, we will move forward in unsanctioned relationships.

We never talk about it, probably because we would view it more as vulgar than honest. However, at the risk of vulgarity, can you imagine the relationships Adam would have had, had he not waited for God to give him someone that was just for him? What if in his haste he mimicked the behavior of the other creatures as opposed to waiting for what God had for him? It is my summation that many of us have been guilty of being with unsanctioned creatures because we could not wait for the hand of God in our lives.

Now, in our haste we have given ourselves to someone or something that will never produce anything that will honor God as it relates to relationship.

It is my belief that a major part of becoming victorious as a single man or woman in the area of sex is to recognize your sexuality. That is not just knowing what you were made for, but also who you were made for. The urges and the desires you have are not sinful; they are a gift from God. Be that as it may, they are gifts that should not be opened or handled by unprepared hands.

This is natural, but it has to be done with the right person. When it is with the right person you do not have to demand anything because their purpose is to serve you in this area as yours is to serve them in the same. If you notice the sacred text in Genesis, God does not give them instructions. He does not have to because it is a proper match; they already know what to do.

The only time this gift becomes tainted is when we try to fulfill it outside of the parameters of God. Holiness does not go out of style. Righteousness is still the order of the day for the believer. We do not get to change God's Word simply because we do not feel like living our lives according to it. Nor do we get to change it because our satiation of our lust has developed a constant craving or addiction. The people of God still have to live a life for God.

Sex is addictive. That's why God set parameters for it. While we cannot really help sexuality, which would be likes, attractions, dislikes, and curiosities, we can help becoming addicted to something to which we should not be addicted.

I am certain that the last paragraph has frightened some. You are now asking what my stand is concerning those who may like the same sex. Well, this is not a work about homosexuality in the church. However, I probably should do one. But this is a work on singles living for God.

I will not argue the legitimacy of the claim of whether or not men and women can be born homosexual. I will only say that the foundation of Christianity has never been how a person was born, but the fact that they can be born again. The Church has become grossly negligent in promoting that message of love and it has left us in a very bitter standoff with those who are homosexual.

Now having said that, I don't care if you are gay or straight, fornication, lust, and adultery are defined the same for every orientation. You still have to honor the Word and will of God if you are a Christian.

To that end please know that sex is indeed an acquired taste (no pun intended). The more you have it, in most cases, the more you will want it. This is a major area of defeat for a great number of Christians, and not just the single ones either.

Countless numbers of homes, marriages, and relationships have all been shattered because of an addiction to sex outside of the parameters that God has set for us. Jobs have been lost, ministries have been ruined, and dreams have been destroyed, all because we have been sexually reckless. Therefore, it is my contention that if we understand our sexuality, it will reduce our chances of falling into sexual sin.

Chapter 5 Quiz

1. What is the difference between Sexuality and Sex?

2. Why is Sexuality so important?

3. When should Sex be experienced?

Chapter 6

What Turns Me On

The assumption is readily made that the only way to know what turns you on is to experience it firsthand, however, this is not true. We should be glad it is not true because that would make God a cruel prankster that only wants to see us fail.

Imagine if I could only know my attractions after I experience them firsthand. That would put me in a place of perpetual failure. That would mean that in order for me to stay away from anything I would have to fall prey to it first. This is simply not true.

The misconception comes from us believing that sex is merely, or at least primarily, a physical act at its core. To the contrary, sex is much more profound than that. The actual act of intercourse is usually a manifestation of what has already been aroused internally. No, not just physiological stimulation, but mentally, emotionally, and spiritually as well.

We have been conditioned by our society and culture to just respond physically, "whatever feels good." Sex, however, is something that involves the total being. That's why it is so devastating when you share yourself with someone only to find out that you are just another number to them. When this happens to Christians we have what the apostle Paul would call "sorrow upon sorrow."

First, there is the spiritual conviction. We feel like we have failed God. We feel like we have fallen short. We even feel the embarrassment of being vulnerable with no one to cover us. Then, there is the personal hurt that is felt from the loss of what we thought for sure was going to be a significant relationship. Unfortunately, if this happens enough we will numb ourselves to begin to function in only shallow, sexual escapades rather than build relationships.

To prevent this, we must stop it before it gets that far. We must understand that sex does not just happen, but there is a process that builds to that moment long before we are physically engaged. We also have to learn that sex, not even good sex, is synonymous with relationship and commitment.

The best way to learn this is by exploring the different levels of attraction.

Mental Attraction

Many feel and promote that attractions are physical first. However, this cannot be further from the truth. In fact, almost all attractions start as mental attractions. I say this because it is impossible to be physically attracted to someone you have not had a physical encounter with. The attraction is really a mental one. You are anticipating the appeal of what you have established attraction to be for you on your personal punch list of attributes you approve. You are actively checking off a list of things that are in your head when you meet a person to decide whether or not you are attracted. This initial attraction is not physical even though you may like what you see physically.

To better illustrate this, in 1988 there was a movie that came out called *I'm Gonna Git You Sucka*. It was a comedy that was written and directed by Keenan Ivory Wayans of the iconic comedic Wayans family. In that movie there is a scene where Keenan's character meets an attractive woman while out. He brings that woman back to a more intimate setting to experience a sexual encounter. As he anxiously awaits this beauty, she begins to dismantle her person. She takes off her hair, her eyelashes, her leg, her butt, and her teeth, and tells him to come on. Clearly, he was not attracted to her. He was attracted to what he thought met the approval of the images of the punch list in his head.

From this I maintain that almost all attractions start off as mental attractions. This is important because this gives us power to choose and not simply react.

Emotional Attraction

This is the stage where attraction becomes deeper. At this stage the other person becomes more than just an acquaintance. You begin to want responsibility for their feelings. You desire to be the one to make them happy. You shoulder the blame for their unhappiness. You feel as though you can guide their emotional state. They will also buy into this and they want you to be responsible for their feelings.

This stage in relationship development is why we are misguided in what "true love" is all about. We as a culture believe that we can define love being authentic by how the other person makes us feel. However, "true love" can only be determined by what we are willing to give to the other person, not how they make us feel.

Spiritual Attraction

Spiritual attraction is deeper than both mental and emotional attraction. This is the level of attraction that causes one to identify with and oftentimes know the other person's innermost feelings and thoughts. It is a deep connection of inner selves. Spiritual attraction is when you enjoy the person because of who they are…period. It does not matter what happens or the obstacles that come up; you are with them because you are committed to another life. You are committed to the person.

*Mental, Emotional, and Physical attractions can all occur without having a Spiritual attraction; however, Spiritual attraction cannot occur without Mental and Emotional attractions preceding it.

Physical Attraction

In logic, a physical attraction can only occur after a physical encounter. By definition, this attraction is physical, meaning it requires physicality. On occasion, when physical attraction or interest is the priority, we are dealing with lust. However, even lust itself is in the heart or the mind long before it is manifested in the flesh.

It is important for us to know how attraction works when we look at what turns us on. I maintain this because if we know how this works we have a better chance of controlling it. Many people are devastated and destroyed by and in relationships that have become a working dysfunction because they don't understand how attraction works and they feel they have no control over their urges, fantasies, and ideologies. To know this is to become empowered.

Almost all attractions start on a mental level. Someone speaking to what you have determined as your need or desire. Long before your flesh gets involved that have been causing you to respond mentally.

The Point of No Return
I can handle it!
I know how to control myself!
I know when to say, "Stop!"

These are all common lines in male/female relationships that we use to give ourselves a false sense of security when we are encountering someone we are attracted to. We believe that we can stop anytime we want. The reality is however, that everyone has a **point of no return.** The problem with the reality is we usually learn where that is after we have reached it. It's usually too late!

The point of no return is hard to know because it can be different every time. There is no real uniformity to it. Because we are human beings and our moods and chemistry are subject to change erratically and/or daily, we never know what point will be our point of no return.

Bereavement, excitement, anger, depression, loneliness, and fatigue are all moods that can alter one's sex drive and ability to be stimulated. Therefore, we have to be aware of what moods cause us more vulnerability than others. It is possible to find yourself in a relationship not because you chose them, but because your sensitivities were manipulated in a mood of vulnerability.

Therefore, we control our situation by never allowing ourselves to get into one that can be manipulated by the other person.

Chapter 6 Quiz

1. Why are all attractions mental first?

2. What is Emotional Attraction?

3. What is Spiritual Attraction?

4. What is Physical Attraction?

_____
_____
_____
_____
_____
_____

5. What is the "Point of No Return"?

_____
_____
_____
_____
_____
_____

Chapter 7

If Walls Could Talk!

There is another taboo among Christians pertaining to sexuality. It is called masturbation. We are uncomfortable talking about it, but that does not dismiss the reality of it.

Perhaps the most stirring question about masturbation is, "Is it right or wrong?" Many hold that masturbation is **nasty** and **perverted.** However, this response usually comes from a lack of knowledge and sexual understanding. The only way we can find out if masturbation is actually sinful is to go to the Word of God.

The Scriptures mention absolutely nothing about this issue. So then, because God is thorough in His help to us with overcoming sin, it is not likely that He forgot to mention one.

Many would list Genesis 38 to refute my stance on the matter. However, Genesis 38 is not about masturbation; it is about *coitus interruptus*. This is when a man enters a woman for the purpose of sexual intercourse but does not want the responsibility of offspring. Therefore, he removes himself and allows the seed to spill as opposed to risking impregnation. This does not definitively address the issue of masturbation. This is saying, "Why would you be doing what produces a baby with someone you don't want a baby with?"

However, the apostle Paul speaks to us candidly about issues like this in the fourteenth chapter of the book of Romans. Paul says, "If a man esteems it within his own heart as unclean, then it is unclean." Paul also says, "That if we partake of anything in doubt we are damned because it is not of faith." "For whatsoever is not of faith is sin." Then there is Paul's greatest statement for any gray area, "… let every man be fully persuaded in his own mind."

The issue is because we do have the Holy Spirit we must exercise prayer and ask Him for guidance on issues like this. Guidance is definitely needed more so than rules. I say this because masturbation is indeed a form of sexual gratification. It is **self-sex**. Therefore, it can be just as addictive and lead to other issues like sexual intercourse can.

Also, we must realize that masturbation is kind of like smelling your favorite food, but not being able to taste it. The question must be asked and seriously considered, will this enhance my desire for sexual intercourse? Or, can I maintain with just this action?

It is necessary for me to also mention that if you have a high sex drive and have been sexually active, masturbation will probably not fill in the gaps with any type of true satisfaction. In many cases, it will push the desire further. Only discipline through prayer can help in this matter. There must be a constant rededication to the Lord so that the habit does not get the best of your existence.

So many people become slaves to their sexual appetites and at the point of addiction, sex is sinful anyway. That's why Paul tells us in 2 Corinthians 10:5 that we have to "cast down imagination and every high thing that exalts itself against the knowledge of God" and what He wants for our lives.

Masturbation is very controversial. People have said it will make you go blind, cross-eyed, and even drive you crazy. Our criminal justice records even show people being arrested for doing it. It is definitely taboo. My personal opinion on the matter is to seek the Lord. However, I must be honest. As a pastor I would rather have people masturbate than to fornicate or commit adultery.

In your prayers you have to be honest. Do not ask God for control over masturbating. Ask God for control of your sexual appetite. I say this because if it were not for the sexual appetite, you probably wouldn't be masturbating in the first place. Ask God to put something in the place of that desire that will help you develop your life as a single person. This could be your education, a business plan, a ministry, or anything that will help you fulfill your goals as an individual until you can fulfill your sexual desires with the person of your dreams.

Chapter 7 Quiz

1. What does Scripture say about Masturbation?

_____
_____
_____
_____
_____
_____

2. What are some true possible risks of Masturbation?

_____
_____
_____
_____
_____
_____

Chapter 8

Saving All My Love

I believe in the discipline of abstinence. As a matter of fact, I feel that if you are a single person, it is the only way to truly please God as it relates to sexual intercourse.

One of the most difficult things to do in this society is to bring our sexual appetites under subjection. Our society uses sex to sell everything. Sex is used for therapy. Sex is used for revenge. Sex is used to celebrate and sex is used to mourn. However, this is not natural; it is a perversion.

Sex should never take the place of conversation, respect, and the human dynamic of interaction. Sex is actually the lowest common denominator. Our society says, "Don't reason...just respond," and we have developed that mentality as our primary place of interaction. Even in our relationships as

Christians we don't reason, we just respond. That response has gotten many of us into trouble, time and time again.

Sex is not an isolated experience, but sex involves the entirety of every human being who indulges in it. Mind, body, and soul are all impacted. No one can simply make love or have sex with just their body. Sex should be understood as a deep, spiritual exchange between two consenting persons. This is why you never forget who you've had sex with. In fact, you won't ever forget the person who you wanted to have sex with because the emotions that are connected to the experience are far too powerful and consuming to just get away from.

Sex is the only way in which two people can actually become one physically. It is the manifestation of the marrying act that has first taken place in the heart. Perhaps this is why so many of us who were sexually active before we had a chance to get married and do it the right way feel as if we have wasted so much time. Time that we will never get back. Many are the adults and young adults that feel wasted from and by the multiple lovers' random sex acts.

Abstinence is the only totally effective way of preventing STDs and pregnancy. Most of all, abstinence is a sure way to develop self-respect and moral standard in a relationship with another person who is supposed to love God.

I also need to add that people who you may be interested in will respect you more for abstaining. I can only speak for men; but, our philosophy is, "Date a freak and marry a lady." No one wants a loose person, whether you're a male or female. We owe it to God and to our mate to save ourselves for them.

With this in mind, I believe in the concept of a *second virginity*. I believe it is possible to set oneself apart for the purpose of consecration and holiness for Christ (even after an active history of sex). Furthermore, I believe that Christ will bless the sacrifice and the effort with the desire of your heart.

To do this is not that difficult. It only requires a made-up mind, a sincere heart, a truly saved mate, and a strong support group of friends. I know it, because my wife and I did it. We really wanted the Lord to bless our marriage. So, we committed ourselves to abstinence. It wasn't the easiest thing I've ever done, but I can testify that it was worth it. I am convinced that us sacrificing our flesh to the Lord is one of the reasons our marriage and ministry have been so blessed.

Contract of Abstinence
For

_____

Lord, I know that I have fallen short of Your glory in the area of sex. I come to You repenting and asking You to forgive me. I understand that You are able to supply all of my needs. Therefore, I turn this part of my life completely over to You. I am asking You to sustain me in my purity for Your glory. Help me to be both an asset and a witness to myself and the Kingdom of God. Help me to stand on the principles of Your Word, Your will, and Your way. I give my body back to You. Amen.

Signature_____

Date_____

Chapter 8 Quiz

1. What is Abstinence?

   _____
   _____
   _____
   _____
   _____

2. How can Abstinence help in building my relationship?

   _____
   _____
   _____
   _____
   _____

3. What is a "Second Virginity"?

   _____
   _____
   _____
   _____
   _____

Chapter 9

Has Anybody Seen "Do Right"?

Since we've ministered to ourselves in the area of knowing self and sexuality, we are actually prepared for dating. It is imperative before we explore dating and courtships that we have a handle on our own existence as a human being. At this point we begin looking for a relationship and have something to offer. Not just things and stuff, but a whole and healthy individual.

That leads me to the question, has anybody seen "Do Right"? "Do Right" is different from person to person. One person's idea of the right person can be totally different from another person's idea of the right person. That's why it's so important to know yourself.

In knowing yourself and what makes you...you, you become clear on what will be a lifestyle for you as it relates to your relationship. More importantly, you are also aware of who you can be a blessing to. That's really an underrated question that should be asked by every single person...who can I be a blessing to? A relationship is not just about you being blessed; it's just as much about you being a blessing to the person you're with.

So, how do we find Do Right? It's simple...by doing right!

First, we must never underestimate the necessity of clear communication in a relationship. It is the foundation of the building. Usually, through effective communicating you can tell right away if the person you are dealing with has even the slightest chance of being Do Right.

Notice, I did not say conversation is the key, but communication. Let's discuss the difference.

The reality is, when people communicate they share the things that make them who they are. Remember, you don't have time to waste jumping in and out of dates and relationships. Dialogue is an issue of the utmost importance.

We also must avoid miscommunications. We need for the person to define what they are talking about when they throw out terms or statements that are very subjective.

Statements That Need Defining

- **I'm old-fashioned.**
- **I'm looking for someone spiritual.**
- **I like someone who's independent.**
- **I believe in trust.**
- **I like an open relationship.**
- **I need to know that I'm the only one.**
- **I need you.**

Also, remember that dating nurtures a relationship. It is a guarantee that the kind of dates you have will be indicative of the kind of relationship you are building. If you don't like the way the dates are going, you will never like the way the relationship will be going.

Because you are a Christian, please remember that dating should be conducive for Christian conduct. You should never have a date that can place you in a compromising predicament.

Some Guideline for Dating

- Who decides where to go?
- What is the norm?
- How are you treated in public?
- How are you treated privately?
- What are the two definitions of a date?
- Who pays?
- Are you the center of their attention?

Chapter 9 Quiz

1. What is Communication?

2. Why is Communication so important?

3. Why should we clarify comments made during dating?

Chapter 10

Decision Time

No relationship should be in a perpetual state of, I DON'T KNOW!

Remember, you don't have time to waste. You don't have plenty of emotions to burn. Therefore, a decision needs to be made about the relationship. Is it a go or is it a no? Stringing people along just for the sake of having something to do is really not fair to anyone involved. This used to be something typical of men, but now women are very guilty of doing the same thing. MAKE A DECISION!

Also, there are many of us who hold on to relationships because of our fears of trying something new. Many people will be miserable in a familiar relationship rather than try being happy in a new one. This is not fair to you or the other person… MAKE A DECISION!

There comes a time when you have done all you can do. You have depleted your storehouse of understanding and second chances. MAKE A DECISION!

Decisions are not always comfortable or easy to make, but they are beneficial. Finally, don't make hasty decisions. Let Philippians 4:6-8 work for you.

Philippians 4:6-8
Be careful for nothing; but in every thing by prayer and supplication with thanksgiving let your requests be made known unto God. And the peace of God, which passeth all understanding, shall keep your hearts and minds through Christ Jesus. Finally, brethren, whatsoever things are true, whatsoever things are honest, whatsoever things are just, whatsoever things are pure, whatsoever things are lovely, whatsoever things are of good report; if there be any virtue, and if there be any praise, think on these things.

You may be one decision away from the relationship God has for you!

In the meantime and in between time, remember that the basic reality of singlehood is you will be single until you're not single. So, do yourself a favor...take the pressure off yourself. You will not be in a fruitful relationship until God directs your paths that way. So, the question becomes, what do I do while I'm single?

1. **Enjoy** – Enjoy your singlehood. Live it to its fullest. Do everything you can do and accomplish everything you can accomplish. Be a whole person as a single person because once you get married, it's forever! Even if you get a divorce...
2. **Engage** – You should be very active. Be involved in life. Be a part of something bigger than yourself. Do things that are appealing to you and do things that help other people. God will not get the glory out of you staying home until you're bored enough to sin (plays, concerts, vacations, school, clubs, and friends are all available and fun).
3. **Entice** – It's not what you think! You have an obligation even as singles to win souls to Christ. The lifestyle you live has to be holy and alluring to do that. Through your witness as a single man or woman people should become enticed to commit to Christ themselves. Singleness should not be a task; it should be a tool. Because you are cute, stylish, fun, intelligent, fair, real,

nonjudging, and encouraging, you will be a human magnet for Christ.

4. **Endure** – As much as we try to convince otherwise, this single and saved stuff can be very difficult at times. Salvation comes with difficulty no matter what one's marital status is. However, we have to endure. There will be times when we stumble and even fall, but we have to be like Paul (Philippians 3:14).

5. **Employ** – You have to employ what you've learned. You must put your experiences and what has been successful for you to work so that you might have a victorious season in your singleness. Lastly, employ your faith. Hebrews 11:6 says without faith it is impossible to please God. Employ your faith in action that might work for you and with you. Your faith in the Lord is powerful enough to transcend any circumstance that you are faced with.

Have Faith!

**TRUST GOD FOR THE LONELY NIGHTS
TRUST GOD FOR THE COMPANION
TRUST GOD FOR THE WILLPOWER
TO ABSTAIN
TRUST GOD FOR GUIDANCE**

HAVE FAITH!

God Bless You!

Chapter 10 Quiz

1. How do I waste time dating?

2. Why is a decision so important?

3. What should I do in the meantime?

Decision Time

4. What five people will I recommend this book to?

_____
_____
_____
_____
_____
_____
_____
_____

About the Author

Bishop Kenneth W. Paramore, DMin., was born the fifth of six boys to James and Betty Paramore. He was reared in Youngstown, Ohio and is a product of the city school system, graduating in 1984 from The Rayen School. He attended the University of Akron on an athletic scholarship and graduated with an associate's degree in criminal justice and Afro-American studies, as well as a bachelor's degree in technical education. Kenneth also holds two master's degrees in counseling: one from Ashland Theological Seminary; and the other from the accredited Bible college he started, the Bradley Bible College, named after his mentor Dr. I. T. Bradley. Kenneth graduated in May of 2015 with doctorate of ministry from United Theological Seminary.

Kenneth is married to the former Leta Marcella Salter. They have been married for twenty-eight years and they have been blessed with two children to their union, Brittne and Kenneth II. Kenneth also has an older daughter, Janaya. Kenneth attributes a great portion of his success in ministry to his very supportive and ministry-minded wife.

While Kenneth has been pastoring since the age of twenty-four, he is certain that the best of God is yet to be. He has been the shepherd of historical churches in Akron, Ohio such as Shiloh Missionary Baptist Church (two years) and the United Baptist Church (fifteen years). He was commissioned by God to plant the Christian Revival and Discipleship Center (now Christ Centered Church) on July 5, 2004. That ministry has grown from eight to well over a thousand members in eleven years. Kenneth attributes the growth to the mercy and grace of God. While holding a plethora of civic awards and accomplishments, Kenneth would rather be known by his ministerial philosophy, "Saving Souls, Salvaging Lives."

In 2014 Kenneth was consecrated to the office of bishop by the Kingdom Connection Fellowship

About the Author

under the leadership of Bishop Jerome H. Ross. He currently serves as the bishop of the College of Ministers and Elders. He is excited about the next chapter of ministry.

Follow Bishop Kenneth W. Paramore, DMin,
in the following ways:

Blog: bishopparamore.blogspot.com
Facebook: Bishop Kenneth Wayne Paramore

To invite Bishop Kenneth W. Paramore
to speak contact:

E-mail: bishopkwp1@gmail.com
Website: trycrdc.org

www.ingramcontent.com/pod-product-compliance
Lightning Source LLC
Chambersburg PA
CBHW060211050426
42446CB00013B/3054